MW00700832

Coming Home
After the Storm

poems of contemplation & stillness

Jennifer Pearson

Copyright © 2021 by Jennifer Pearson

jen@snowytree.com

All rights reserved.

ISBN 978-1-949053-12-8

Pinecone Book Company
Colorado USA

To Mary Oliver,
Naomi Shahib Nye,
Billy Collins,
Rumi,
and Thich Nhat Hanh
whose poetry
inspires me daily.

CONTENTS

Part I: Slightest Cool Breeze

Part II: Honey from a Star Thistle

Part III: Unsavory Bits

Part IV: Safely in My Dinghy

Part V: No Big Deal

PART I
Slightest Cool Breeze

Looking for the Moon

When sleep eludes me
And it's still
The darkest of night,
I sleep walk through my house
Looking for the moon
To surprise me
Through one of the many windows.

Something about the moon
Calms me,
Helps me to believe
That all is as it should
Be, in this very moment.

Maybe it's the phases
Of the moon
And its relationship to the
Allusiveness
Of time?

A celestial clock
Revealing
The turning of the earth,
The moving of our lives,
The aging of all things.

Slowly
I make my way back,
Legs heavy,
To the cozy blankets,
Into a peaceful
Slumber.

Compost

Oh, us humans,
like ants on a mammoth mound
plodding toward perfection.

Yet, the heavy sense of unease
looms around each bend,
so we wonder,
"Why even try?"

What if ...
 the troubles of
 life are simply the path
 to truth?

What if...
 the confusion
 is the very condition
 for growth?

What if ...
 suffering is the compost,
 pain is the fertilizer
 for our awakening?

Let's allow
ourselves to settle
more deeply into this
grand adventure of
not knowing.

As the ants march
over the ground
not knowing the
bigger picture of their
existence,
so do we.

Quarantine Haiku 1

The world looks crazy
My practice grows full of grace
Dragonflies dart 'round

Quarantine Haiku 2

Fear creeps into now
People are selfish, confused
About the future

Quarantine Haiku 3

Slow moving forward
Taking care of each other
Is the only path

Quarantine Haiku 4

Pain and suffering
Abound, be present, connect
Through calm, we come home

Cricket

As I sit in my garden
Observing a cricket
In her last moments
Of life.

I instinctively want to save it
Feeling the tightening of my chest
In the face of death.

I allow that thought
To pass by
As I watch this
Extraordinary creature
With long antennae
Slip back to the earth.

I am a witness
To this noble being
In its profound last seconds
Knowing that
This will also be me
One day.

Unafraid,
I breathe a deep breath,
She breathing her last,
Our breath blends
We inter-are.

Buzzzzzzzz

The racer striped
Honey bee glides
From dandelion to thistle,
Buzz, buzz, buzz
And my heart quickens.

Chest tightening as it gets
Closer and louder
Fear and curiosity intermingle
With awe.

Will it sting me?
My mind stutters
No...
wait...
Yes...
wait...
Maybe.

The honey bee casually
Flies away with
No thought of me at all.
Searching for
Sweet clover and alfalfa
As it goes about its day.

I suppose that's the
Way of fear,
Moving through our bodies
Onto the next.

Night Walk in Winter

my cheeks get that certain
color of red
burnt sienna
crimson

as my breath appears like mist
head and hands covered with
a beloved
hat and mittens

everything looks
a bit foreboding
in the pitch black
of night

the shimmer on the road reveals
newly melted snow
reflected by the
waning crescent moon

we cuddle together
arm in arm
in silence
taking it all in

there is an intense
intimacy that exists in
this cold dark
silent space

always a struggle to leave
our cozy warm
home for the frigid air and
uncertainty of night

but I am consistently
rewarded with
just a bit of magic
in the brisk evening

stars overhead
and the deepest stillness

Ripples

A pebble
tossed into the still water
breaks the silence,
the unbearable
alluring
silence.

Ripples
cross the still water,
moving to the shore,
from the shore
rocking back
and forth.

Ripples
are words spoken
between friends,
carefully or not,
extending outward
and onward.

The gentle touch
and eye contact,
connections,
allowing another to be
seen and heard.

Mindful of each ripple
as we change
the world
with each small act
in each and every moment.

Four Season Mountain Haiku

winter fills my mind
swirling wind shaped ice sculptures
sparkling snow crystals

northern flickers call
out, springtime in the rockies
rivers thaw, snow melts

summer cicadas
sing as we sit by the fire
stars twinkle at night

Red tailed hawks circle
High above the snowy peaks
As Aspen leaves fall

Pinprick

some peace that lives
deep
in the soul
that comes alive like a
pinprick
of exhilaration

the gentle
brisk breeze
that brings a
slight shiver
across my whole
body

maybe
in that moment
i am the most alive
the most
interconnected
to all

there is a knowing of
never being alone

Water

From the rainwater
strolling down the rusted gutter
on the side of a old red
weathered farmhouse
filling the barrel
for later use

To the creek snaking
its way
under the ice
in the coldness of winter
hidden but roaring in
the silence of snow

From the ripples lapping
at the sand
with subtle sounds
of calm
allowing my breath to
synchronize

To the waterfall
off the beaten path
making its way from
high snowy peaks
through sticks and rocks
gradually
yet powerfully
carving the earth

Field Mice

We have been catching
Small voles under our sink
Then releasing them two miles away.

I wonder how they might find
Their way back home?

As they explore the container,
I drive them to the field near
Our home.

Upon release,
One is tiny and hiding,
Very shy but, ultimately,
Curious enough
To inch out of the container.

Another,
Its nose twitching in
The cool fall air,
Dashing quickly into
The high grass.

Still another,
Is very petite, peering out
To see if it's safe,
Creeping over to the grass,
Hoping not to be seen.

Each one seeing the world
From a different perspective.
I can't help but
See our diverse humanity
Reflected.

Wild Horses

Do they calm by tying them
tightly to a fence
or
by giving them a large area
to roam and be free?

Your mind is like the wild horse,
it calms when it feels safe
slowly over time.

The horse responds
to loving touch,
to calm breathing,
to slow movements,
to kind words,

so do you.

Never wholly tamed or
predictable,
that's the intrigue.
Always keeping you
on your toes.
Never knowing for sure when it
might buck
and run free.

Make a friend
of your mind,
in times of peace,
in times of agitation,
remembering always,
it's the nature of mind
to roam
just like the wild horse.
Unpredictably.

Lazy Days

The lazy days of summer
stretching in the heat of the afternoon,
cat
stretches
too.

The air is still, hot, and sticky
making me tired and slow
imagining my body like a
huge
Galapagos
turtle.

Gulping down ice cold water
as if on a desert island
water leaking from the corners of my mouth
the cold shocking but feeling
oooh
so
lovely.

Remembering my ancestors
in Mississippi waking before dawn
before the blistering heat
rocking back and forth in the afternoon
on the massive veranda
bigger than the house
trying not to
move
a
muscle.

As my day rolls by
the Colorado air cools
breezes blow gently
across the hairs on my arm
wrapping a shawl
over my shoulders
sighing as the
stars
emerge
overhead.

What a World

to go to sleep in heavy heat,
wildfire smoke seeping
through the floorboards
and window gaps,
seeping under my covers
as if a nagging
unanswerable question
lingered in the air.

this morning, I awoke
to such delight
to brisk morning air
a light blanket of snow
on each still green aspen leaf.

drinking chamomile tea
when it is cold,
what a pleasure to behold
steam rising from my cup,
a cold breeze seeping
through the old pane.

when I remember
this moment,
some time
in the future,
i imagine smiling
inwardly
holding a delightful secret.

Mountain

Reaching the top
Of the mountain

The poet within
Becomes mute

Surrounded by
Verse without
Words

PART II
Honey from a Star Thistle

Shower Meditation

Readying myself
For a hot shower
As the snow piles up
Outside my window.

Undressing
Stepping into the water
Placing my whole head
Under the shower.

Imagining a waterfall
In the dense jungle
Sounds of wild animals
Abound.

Loud chirps and trills of
Yellow banded poison dart frogs,
Monkeys howling above in the trees,
Cicada's singing their high-pitched song.

I am fully present
Empty of all desire
To be anywhere but here
With the steam and the soap.

Surprised as I feel
The water begin to get cold,
Gently opening my eyes
With a rye smile
Ready for this day.

Unique Moment

I watched the rain,
turn to snow
then rain again
steadily falling on
the lilac blossoms outside
my
window.

The cat and I sit
very still
knowing that
any movement
might
disturb
the stillness of this
precious moment.

I drink in the quiet
like a warm cup of jasmine tea,
slow and gratefully,
wanting to linger longer
but knowing
that this moment,
as with each moment
is unique.

The Dalai Lama's Laugh

Are there any noises
Quite so contagious
As his Holiness's laugh?
Just thinking about it
Invites a giggle in my belly.

If you want to
Join me, right now
Allow a smile
To cross your face.

There is a joy in smiling
That resides deep in our hearts
And spreads
Through each cell of our body.

Allowing the tingle to
Travel from your toes
To the top of your head.

Let it flow
Like a white water river
Curling and touching
Each person that you meet
With a spark of kindness.

Imagine, just for an instant,
What the world
Would be
If every one of us
Spent some small
Portion of each day
Trying to spread
The Dalai Lama's laugh?

Breakfast Discussion

"Shall we take down the sign?"
My husband asks casually
Over scrambled eggs.
The one out front saying,
BLACK LIVES MATTER,
In big bold letters.

I am silent but
Inside cry,
"NO WAY
The work has just begun."

We cannot take it down until
Institutionalized racism is recognized
And changing.

We cannot take it down
Until we have at least one year
When no people of color are killed
By the very people
Who are supposed to protect them.

We cannot take it down,
Well,
Maybe ever.

Taking it down would say,
Let's go back to the way it used to be.

Taking it down would say,
Let's go back to sleep at the wheel.

We must
NEVER
Fall asleep
Again,
The wake up calls are way,
Way too painful.

I say to my kind husband,
"Let's keep it up,
I really like it there."
"OK," he says.

Between Asleep and Awake

There is this time
between asleep and awake
where there is
    no me
    no ego
    no self
dissolving into a million little pieces
spread around the globe
transcending time and place

I am a hurricane rising in the Atlantic
    so powerful that I can knock down
    houses and trees

I am a pharaoh from ancient Egypt
    spending eternity in a pyramid

I am riding on a shooting star
    through the galaxies
    just to see what i can see

I am a monk living in the forests of Burma
    noticing every little breeze and bug

I am a nurse treating the wounded in WWII
    healing people on the outside and inside

I am a 200-year-old eucalyptus tree
    reaching so high that
    I can touch the sky
    spreading healing scents with each
    gust of California wind

I am the whole universe contained
    in one small smile

I am you, you are me

Breathe

As I feel my body rise and fall,
I hold gratitude for my ability
To simply breathe.

So many cannot,
The smoker with the hacking cough
That won't ever give her a moment's rest.

The grizzled, old man who spent his life
Working in the mines
Like many generations before.

The young man murdered by police
While they stood on his neck,
"I cannot breathe".

The firefighters who
Risk their lives
While their lungs fill with smoke.

I meditate daily with
Breath as my anchor,
Relishing the gift of the air
flowing in and out,
Knowing that it will not
always
be
so.

Contradiction

Human beings can be
like tangles of vines
holding sneaky,
invisible,
barbs.

Truth hides,
sneaking around;
sometimes clear
then quickly muddled
a pebble thrown into
a still pond.

Truth must withstand
the changing tides
of thought and feeling
until, with patience,
it holds steady.

This may take a while.
as we grow weary,
tired of fighting.

Constantly holding such
contradictions
can exhaust our
human soul.

But love is simple -
carrying safety, beauty,
and kindness as
surprising
stowaways.

What Do You Do When...

The people who are supposed to love you
keep kicking you when you are down.

The kinder you are,
the meaner they are.

You put on a smile everyday with hope
but face daily sorrow in your children's eyes.

You work at meaningless jobs to pay the bills
but the bills never get paid.

You hold loving kindness in your heart
yet, quickly feel it drain away with exhaustion.

I suppose the only thing you can do ...

Find peace in the water
as it washes over you in the shower.

Count the spots
on the back of the ladybug.

Help your demented neighbor
find her way home.

Enjoy the rice
in your bowl.

Breathe deeply into the scent
after it rains.

Watch the chickadee drink the rainwater
From a leaf.

Remember the holiness that
exists everywhere.

This Body

This body with
Flab
where there once was muscle
Bumps
where it once was flat
Wrinkles
where it once was smooth
Scars
where there once was innocence

This body
weathering the storms
sturdy through it all

This body
both broken and perfect
holding a lifetime of memories

This body
breathing with predictability
as it steadily rises and falls

This body
alive with each warm breeze
with each back ache
with each kind touch

Crummy Days

Low, sad, boring days
These days just have to happen,
I suppose.

In the middle of the most
Dreadful day,
Clinging to the apathy
Like a security blanket.
My body,
Heavy,
Refusing to move.

What if
I simply allow,
Hold this discomfort
like a sleeping child,
Not fighting anymore.

A little breathing,
A little intention,
Melancholy lifts a bit,
Stretching my arms over my head,
Feel my feet on the earth,
Then begin to
Look toward
Tomorrow.

Part III
Unsavory Bits

Expiration Date

what might you notice
if you knew your expiration
date?
the dust bunnies in the corner
the neighbor laughing
the crack in the sidewalk

would you
travel to Iceland or Ireland,
scream loudly not caring who hears,
connect with people deeply,
ride your bike,
sit in your same comfy chair,
eat Ben and Jerry's cherry garcia ice cream
for hours,
slowly savoring every bite,
make amends,
clean the house,
notice all the sounds in nature

i think i would
keep my secret,
spend the day reading poetry under
the beautiful willow tree
next to the small pond
with my people
sharing bits of our books
that make us smile

i would have my soft blanket
and slowly disappear
into the great mystery

snapshot

A man across the room
vigorously cleans off his table,
sips his coffee with trembling hands
in this dilapidated coffee shop.

He picks up his novel,
as his eyes dart around nervously
seemingly, unaware
of me watching him.

What if,
he is a detective
hired to follow someone
who is
cheating on their spouse or
embezzling money?

Or possibly,
he's grieving after
the death of his wife,
this coffee shop holding
warm memories
of their life together.

Or maybe,
he's a poet,
like me,
observing me
as I observe him.

Writing...
"middle aged woman with notebook
pretending to read."

All of us held
in this small snapshot.

Seeker

Is it goodness that we seek?
Or kindness
Or meaning
Or peace?

What needs to exist to give us
The life
That we want?

We shift like swallows
Angling quickly in the air.

One minute
wanting connection.
Next minute
wanting to be alone
Next minute
Wanting to make the world
A better place.
Next minute
Simply wanting to have fun.
Next minute
Wanting to make enough money.
Next minute
Wanting a simple life.

Ultimately, it is simple.

We want to enjoy
The people who we love.
And not get snagged
In always wanting
What we do not have.

Poet's Eyes

reading mary oliver
billy collins
naomi shihab nye
inspires me
to dig deep into metaphor
into nature itself

to look a little askew
at the goings on
of daily life

see with curiosity
the whats and the whys
of consciousness

to watch people in the grocery
with poets eyes
the creek at the end of the road
with wonder
the field of grass swaying in the wind
with awe

looking with these eyes
makes all of life a poem.

Lottery

Sometimes I forget about
How I got here.

The arbitrary genetic lottery
That has granted my life.

I wonder about who I would be
If another path claimed me.

If my son was taken by war
as a boy?

If I needed to work
Two jobs as a single parent?

If I was a royal servant
at a palace in Baghdad?

If I was a curious young
woman in Afganistan?

My mind creating
fiction
out of possibilities
makes my head spin.

Then I take refuge in the life
That was given
And I am present.

Beachside Cafe

Outside with the buzz of
Conversation all around
I sit alone

Breezes coming off the bay
Pelicans scooping up fish in
Their prehistoric bills

Sailboats anchored riding the
Constant small swells as
Bottlenose dolphin meander
And manatees lumber in the
Tepid waters

Children playing
Laughing in the sand
Skipping rocks on the water
Counting each skip aloud
One, two, three
Such joy held in their small bodies

Kayakers emerge from
The mangrove forests
Relieved after getting lost
In its tangles

I breathe deeply
In communion
With it all

Sacred Spaces

exploring sacred spaces
around the world
brings out the poet in me

time to sit in each and every church
to be in a place where hundreds
of others have prayed,
in joy and sorrow

who moved each of these stones?
who created each pane of stained glass?
who built the bench upon which I sit?
who sat praying for relief from suffering?

could be a mosque, temple,
cathedral, monastery

places where we go
to be honest
to be healed
to be heard

places where
we are fragile and intimate
places where
we connect deeply as one

where we understand
that the sacred exists
in relationship to
one another
in relationship to
ourselves

Vibrantly Flawed

we travel through our
whole lives
thinking,
if I just fixed myself,
then I could be lovable

this brings a
hollow separateness
and loneliness
to our lives

it means that
somehow
we think that there is such a
thing as an
unbroken person

it means that we believe the lie
that we all do not suffer

vibrantly flawed
my tea mug says
down the side

the key is to carry our flaws
crawl inside them
understand them as
an essential
part to our very
humanity

the perfection that
we attempt to
show to the world
is exactly what isolates us
and makes us feel alone

that is the unnatural skin
that makes us feel insincere
the paradox exists everywhere

what we cling to
is exactly what makes us feel
unsafe.

so...
show me your warts
and unsavory bits
that truly make you human

i'll show you mine
these are the connectors
that honestly
define our true selves

Gems

Friendship dissolves time as
sugar in water,
with clarity
and sweetness.

The ones who make you laugh,
who push you to become kinder,
gentler,
who help you live without fear.

The ones who
break the rules with you or
who strengthen
your character.

The ones who you want
never to break from
even after
hours of conversation.

And whose smile fills your soul,
who allow you to be vulnerable,
who bring ease
just with the sight of them.

The ones who are full of
integrity
And those who are full of
contradictions.

All of them teachers,
you never know when one will
find you,
we must keep open,
looking, forgiving,
allowing imperfections.

Zen death poems are traditionally short poems written by Samurai or Zen monks in their final days before death. I was inspired after reading the book *Japanese Death Poems: Written by Zen Monks and Haiku Poets on the Verge of Death.* I was brought into the process by writing these poems early in the morning when the self is not quite alert and awake, imagining how it might be before my own death.

Death poem 1

Body broken
Spirit free
I open my heart to what is next
Shall I be the lotus
Or the mud
The fast flowing river
Or dew on a blade of grass
Let all be
As it will.

Death poem 2

As my mind stills
She comes in
Seeing all in one raindrop
The grandest of trees
And the vulnerability
Of the smallest daisy
As death circles
I am lost in the
No self
And interconnection
Of all

Death poem 3

My skin becomes tingly
Chill bumps rise
As a breeze gently
Blows by
Just as life
Impermanent
Here and gone
Always present
In all that is around me
Never present
With all of the world

Death poem 4

Watching the fly
Slowly die
On the window ledge
With a loud buzz
I know that this is me
Spitting my last breath
Forgetting the inter-are
Clinging to life
Until the last second
Then allowing freedom
To overtake me
As I blend into the
Beauty with the fly
With the billions of
sentient beings
that have gone before.

PART IV
Safely in My Dinghy

Stream of life

A stream carried me
in meditation today
allowing me to glide safely
in my worn, wooden dinghy.

The current may be
swift or slow,
the water
deep or shallow,
impeded by
old sticks,
sediment, and stones.

Some thoughts flow,
some cling,
as the rush of my river goes,
i am free, life simply moves
i am both in it and not.

I smile in my dinghy
as curiosity carries me
around the next bend.

Kindness

When I awake to anger,
I implore kindness to channel my rage.

When I awake to sadness,
I allow kindness to fill my soul.

When I awake to fear,
I am still, as kindness calms my mind.

When I awake to frustration,
I ask kindness to sit by my side.

When I awake to hopelessness,
I urge kindness to open my heart.

With practice,
it only takes a moment
before tears of gratitude
slip down my cheeks.

I cannot
change another,
therefore I strive to
change myself.

Solitude

"The cure to loneliness is solitude." ~ Marianne Moore

Alone is quiet and beautiful
Without suffering.

Isolation is not a choice,
Beseeching others to bring comfort.

Withdrawal begs for discovery.

Peace brings deep and fulfilling breath
That calms the body.

Emptiness is simply being
In this present moment
with no expectations.

Solitude is full of pleasure
The skin
Quivering with possibilities.

Wilderness allows all
Inner self to be Ok.

Retreat allows me to disappear
And become us.

Leaning

leaning against a tree
in the local park
the sun warms my face

the last withered
leaves fall
on the still green grass

few people wandering
some noticing me
others hurrying by

my breath is calm
moving in and out
as my chest rises and falls

my breath mingles
and dances like smoke
in the cool autumn air

the deer at the edge
of the forest
breathing the same air

both feeling
anchored and safe
in nature's spell

Why I Meditate

To feel the breath in my body
open my heart like a giant sunflower

Because I suffer.

To fill the longing for spirituality
To keep dementia at bay
To boost my immune system
To be kinder, the kindness that comes only with practice

Because life's too short and I relish slowing down.

To choose love over fear
To make generosity a habit
To be amazed by the changing of each season
To smile more

Because as I grow older, I am more comfortable with
emptiness.

To build bridges
To fall in love with my old broken body
To make all the green in the world more vibrant
To simply feel gratitude deep in my bones
        Even for the spiders
        Even for the cracks
        Even for the grief

Silent Retreat

The silence that many fear
is my coziest and safest of places.
Often my mind runs me
ragged from one crazy story to the next
but that's ok.

Layers of ego,
slowly vaporize like morning fog
off a still lake.
Allowing each moment
to become truly mindful,
all of us
uniting in silence.

Allowing forgiveness
to expand,
thoughts and feelings
simply exist
without stories running around
like kids out for recess.

Stillness inhabiting the
deepest recesses of
my body.
My heart
so full it might
burst with gratitude.

The problem arises
As I reenter the world.

The one in line to get a sandwich
who pushes his way to the
front of the line
unkind and unaware.

My heart beats
a little faster,
my hard exterior
begins to build,
digging deep to see
he as me.

Each return trip from retreat,
I am able to hold
the love for myself and
all humanity,
more strongly,
more deeply,
more humorously.

Dusk

dusk astonishes me
with the colors shifting
second to second
trees becoming silhouettes
against the fading sky

each evening
both different
and the same
clouds holding sunlight after
the sun has been swallowed
by the horizon

colors all then fade
the first stars shine
the crescent moon appears
just a sliver

then
the blue hour
this breathtaking color that
fades to black

M&M Meditation

Do you rip open the bag
Pouring them directly into your mouth quickly,
Feeling all the colored marbles float around,
Crunching many at once
Until they disappear quickly leaving pieces in your teeth
That you root out with your tongue
While watching TV?

OR

Do you separate each bag into piles of colors?
Eating your least favorite colors first,
Brown, orange, blue, yellow, red,
And savoring the beautiful green.

OR

Do you enjoy the color,
Texture, taste,
Of each small and complex
Morsel.
Sometimes it can take
An hour.
Sucking the hard candy coating,
As the chocolate
Melts on your tongue.
Your grin spreading widely
As the texture
Of the peanut comes through.
The peanut breaking apart
Then with the final few crunches,
swallowing satisfied.

Then move to the next.
Always a surprise what color
will roll out.

Heart Break

When I think of you
my heart breaks for the
tightness
in your chest.

The anger and fear that
emanate
from your inner self,
make me want to hold you so
tightly
that you will break open
so completely
that your only
response can be
to love yourself.

I have a sense of the
landscape of your pain,
sometimes made of
rugged dry,
parched earth.

Other times,
torrential down pouring
of rain
that will not let up,
flooding
all the land.

Sometimes I can feel
your suffering as though
it was my own.

The weight on your heart
grows with the vividness
of your fear.

I want to bathe you
in love and peace.

May you be free from suffering.
May you be held in compassion.
May you know peace.

Sometimes

mindfulness arrives with ease
into the dawning of another
delightful morning.

waking as the sun
begins to lighten my room,
stretching my body
sliding my socked feet
on the wood floor.

sitting on my cushion
my blanket,
that once held my mother,
holding me tenderly
as I sit and smile
and breathe.

other times…
I startle awake
worrying,
heart racing.

the sun is bright
through my window
as I squint, feeling hurried.

wait, wait
a quiet voice says,
slow down,
slow down,
all is well.

calming my breath
eyeing my meditation space,
gently nudge
myself to sit,
just a bit.

the practice
settles in quickly
i sit and breathe,
coming home
after a storm.

A Really Good Day

A 6 year old
Watches the frog hopping
Around the small pond
As though there is nothing else
in the world.

Wonder at the sliminess,
The jumpiness,
The croak and ribbit
Absorbs her completely.

The frog jumps and jumps,
Followed by this child of wonder.
So attentive,
Until...

She notices
In the distance
A dandelion
In full white,
Ready to be blown,
As she picks the dandelion,
A gust of wind comes
And blows the seeds
Far across the field
Before her.

Dropping the stem,
She chases the seeds,
Laughing,
Jumping,
Running,
Trying to catch them
As they rise higher and
Higher on the breeze.

Then
She collapses into the
Tall green grass,
The warmth of
A midsummer day
Shining on her innocent face.

Breathing heavily,
Red cheeked,
Watching the clouds go by
Describing their shapes
Out loud to herself
Elephant,
Heart,
Wave,
Mustache,
She giggles.

Fireflies

Sometimes it feels as though
My light has gone out
Like a firefly floating around the
Twilight woods
Not knowing how
To flip the switch again.

Searching for the light
In far reaching places
In campfires by the stream
In porch lights
On the farmhouse veranda
In gas lights along
The Seine
In the multitude of lights
Creating a bubble over the city

What she forgot
Was that it can only be relit
From the inside out
The only path that can lead home is
The path of self-compassion.

With this realization
The firefly glows brighter
Than ever before
And helps to
Spark other fireflies
Around the globe.

PART V
No Big Deal

Humbled

From the wind
      sailing a plastic bag
      Into the air on a grimy city street.
To a young man
      kneeling while offering a homemade burrito
      to a homeless man on that same street.

From the snow laying gently
      on a green leaf
      in the late autumn breeze.
To an egg falling
      out of the nest,
      crashing onto the rock below.

From an old woman
      on arthritic knees in the cathedral
      mumbling the rosary.
To the red tail hawk
      circling high above catching thermals
      with its expansive wings.

From a man protecting
      his small child from the elements
      with his large body.
To the vibrant orange sunset
      made from uncontained forest fires
      across the country.

Life brings poetry,
I am humbled by each.

Sleeping in the Desert

A tent sleeper from the midwest
With morning dew
Mosquitoes
Moths
And various other annoyances that
Can keep you awake.

Little did I know
The freedom
Of sleeping in the desert
Under the stars.

Waking to the black moonless night skies,
Shooting stars abundant
No trees or clouds
Blocking the vastness
Of the milky way.

Of course,
The scorpions could burrow
Into our sleeping bags
And maybe a snake
But when your young
And free
Fear holds less of a grip

One Day Soon

This Being Human
Is not such a simple task.
Bombarded by
Thoughts, feelings, noises, smells
Coming from all directions.

Finding small moments of calm
Interspersed with assaults from
Other humans,
From ourselves.

Just trying to get through
Alive, sputtering, as though
Holding our breath is the
Only way out.

Such similarity to our ancient ancestors
Afraid of saber tooth tigers,
Huddling in the cave
Wondering,
Worrying, what's next?

Always looking for tomorrow,
Hoping that
One day we will be at peace,
One day the fog will lift.

Walking through this life pretending,
"No big deal,
Just being human
On this crazy and inexplicable planet."

Mumbai Meditation

Many people
Bustling around
Our sangha meeting place
For our weekly meditation
In my small tent

Noticing
The beeping horns
Laughing children
Music coming from all over
Wafting scents of spices in the air
The small herb garden my wife grows

I sit on a cushion
On the dirt
With friends who smile
Easily

Our eyes close
The distractions
Slide into the background
Of our consciousness
Our breath lengthens and
Slows.

The two human longings
Of freedom and safety
Join together
In my heart and body
I have truly come home.

The singing bowl rings
The sound of life comes
Rushing back into my senses
My smile continues.

I bow to my friends
And we move through
The rest of our day.

My Wish for You Is

that you awake to clean air
each morning

to see in each grapefruit slice an intricacy
surpassed only by the web of a spider

that you find wonder and amusement
in your own unique mind

My wish for you is

that you see beauty in the shape
of your nose, mouth, and eyes

that your fear of the world subsides
and is replaced by equanimity

that you are fully entertained by
the caterpillar devouring the leaf

My wish for you is

to hold joy and suffering
together

to fall in love with the world
over and over again

to enjoy the being
instead of the having

Sorrow

he wept in my arms
as the waves of emotion
released little by little

his shoulders rattled
as my arms held tightly
around his broken memories

how do we share such
pain that shakes us
to the core?

how do we hold it
and travel alone
in the darkness?

love is the net
that can hold
us all

let's go together
rather than allow fear
to keep us apart

The Many Me's

All true and real.

The one who enjoys solitude,
As the river rushes by.

The one who laughs with her whole body,
Living in this precious moment.

The one who lends
Compassionate language
To others in pain.

The one who expresses anger,
And then is full of regret.

The one who seeks truth
From insight, mindfulness, and silence.

The one who holds guilt and shame
From ego and selfishness.

The one who is a good friend
In times of sorrow and joy.

The one who demands the center of attention
Rather than holding the safe space for another.

The one who offers the coat off her back
Without even thinking.

Feeling authentic in each skin
Instead of attaching to one in particular.

Remembering that self and no-self
Reflect one another.

To Really Feel

Loving kindness
Deep within my heart
For the world
For each other
Can make my heart
Break open
With mercy

To feel the empty room
In myself fill
Like a tidal wave
With compassion
For the heart
Of human suffering
Makes
Me feel at one
With each and every
Being

The Stories We Tell

"Have I wasted my life?"
Is the fear of humanity.
Bouncing between,
Too busy,
Not busy enough.
Worried always
Am I enough?

Little lies
Tools to make us look good to others,
While we
Are all trying to pad our
Scorecards.

Just yesterday,
I puffed up and padded
My own story to impress another.

What's crazy is that we
Know when we are deceitful.
But still we believe our own
Swayed stories.

Ego driven,
This comparison game,
At the end of the day,
Is the root of all suffering.

It manages to squirm
Like a virus
Into each thought,
Each action.
Even in the aware ones.
Even in the enlightened ones.

Heaven

We humans
Are remarkable,
We truly are.
But only in these bodies?
Meeting the same people
after we die?

Aren't we simply visitors
Observing daily miracles,
Trying to take care
To leave the earth better
For the next visitors.
A small dew drop
In the whole mystery.

I so much more enjoy
The thought of death being
A constant intermingling
With the rivers
Or the cosmos.

Trying to imagine things
Beyond our perceptions
Is so fascinating.

Even the possibility
That life is so utterly
Priceless
Because we only get one.

Maybe this one
Precious life
Is heaven?

Plant Names

when your mind scurries down
paths of regret
or rivers of self-destruction

begin reciting plant names
seagrass
delphinium
chestnut tree
tulip
morning glory

remember that you
can only hold
one thought at a time

palm tree
bamboo
algae
aloe vera
desert paintbrush.

scour the deep recesses
of your mind for

calla lily
monkey puzzle
baobab
jasmine
mint

then breathe into
your true home

Standing in Venice

Standing in Venice
with the canals flowing by,
thinking about this city's
many incarnations
over hundreds of years.

Refugees from nearby lands
fishing for their daily meal,
escaping the destruction of their
home lands,
due to the ravages of war,
seeking safety.

Traders from
the Middle East and Africa,
Europe and China,
bargaining loudly over
black, red, and white peppercorns
and vibrantly colored silk,
the smell of
wine and spices
filling the market place.

The similar hustle and bustle now,
people from each part
of our planet,
bargaining for Murano glass,
eating black squid ink pasta.

I simply watch
the curious sights
and the sparkling lights
reflecting off
the grand canal.

People taking selfies,
lovers caressing,
friends laughing,
a woman sipping
her cappuccino.

I offer to take a picture for
a couple of tourists,
just like me.

Grandmother's Hands

Her hands where gnarled with arthritis
After years of
Sewing clothes for our barbies,
Peeling hundreds of oranges for ambrosia,
Forced to write as a right hander.
I used to watch those hands and
Listen to her stories.

Now I look at my own hands with wonder.
The age spots coming slowly,
The wrinkles settling in,
The nails thinning,
The joints that have not yet swelled.

Sometimes I cannot believe
That these hands are mine,
Other times
I am so grateful for all
They have done for me.

Writing poems,
Throwing pots,
Holding hands,
Lifting children,
Cooking meals,
Peeling oranges,
Planting gardens.

Then I understand
My hands are
My grandmother's hands.

Made in the USA
Columbia, SC
01 November 2021

48059611R00055